FIX &
FORGET

50 Slow Cooker Recipes

TEST KITCHENS SUPERVISOR–PAT MORRISON
PHOTOGRAPHER–RON OATNEY
RECIPE DEVELOPMENT–JOANNE KARLSON
FOOD STYLIST–JOANNE KARLSON
RECIPE EDITOR–ELAINE GREEN
BOOK DESIGNER–JENNIFER RUBICK

USING YOUR SLOW COOKER

Do you wish there were a way to have dinner almost ready when you get home from work or carpooling? Would you like to cut down your time in the kitchen on weekends, yet have some delicious "home-cooked" meals for your family and friends? Then it's time to dust off your slow cooker. If it can't be found, browse through the new models on the market. You'll be pleased to see that for a modest investment you can own an attractive appliance that may prove to be one of your best kitchen purchases.

Read the information on this page and the following pages plus your owner's manual to help you get to know your slow cooker better. Then turn to the recipes to see how versatile your meals can be!

TIME SAVING TIPS

• Peel and chop the vegetables the night before; cover and refrigerate.

• The night before, trim fat from meat and cut meat into the desired size pieces; cover and refrigerate.

• Thaw frozen vegetables and meat in the refrigerator, OR use your microwave, OR run hot tap water over the package to partially thaw; drain well before using.

• Brown meat according to the recipe directions. Notice that many of our recipes save preparation time by not browning the meat. Did you know that meat will brown more quickly if pieces are not crowded in the skillet and if you cook over medium or medium-high heat? However, if you omit the browning step as stated in a recipe, you must allow for a longer cooking time to be sure the meat is done.

• Since chicken and ground beef cook quickly in the slow cooker, these recipes are especially good for weekends and shorter cooking periods.

• Serve cooked food from your slow cooker or its removable liner to save washing extra dishes.

FREQUENTLY USED TECHNIQUES

• Slow simmering produces a mellow blending of flavors, but whole herbs and spices may give more flavor than usual, while ground herbs and spices may give less flavor. You may want to taste for additional seasoning before serving. Remember to remove bay leaves and whole peppercorns before serving.

• Some vegetables, especially carrots and onions, often take longer to cook than the meat. Place them in the bottom or along the sides of the cooker and cover with liquid which helps the food to cook more quickly. Ingredients are often layered in a specific order with longer cooking ingredients placed in the bottom where they will cook faster and be done with the rest of the ingredients. Stir only if the recipe tells you to.

Pictured on the cover: Garden Chicken Dinner (see page 23).

FREQUENTLY USED TECHNIQUES (CONTINUED)

• To assure even cooking of meat, be sure there is some space between the pieces to allow for circulation of heat and seasonings.

• Both regular and quick-cooking rice need 4 to 5 hours to cook on low. On the high setting, it will take at least 2 hours. You may prefer to cook the rice on the stove, then stir into the mixture about 30 minutes before the end of the cooking time to heat through.

• Pasta needs stirring while cooking to prevent the pieces from sticking together. It is best to cook the pasta separately just until tender, then drain well before stirring into the cooked mixture. The pasta will not overcook if added at the end of the cooking time.

• Tender vegetables such as fresh mushrooms, tomatoes or zucchini will only need to be added for the last 30 to 45 minutes of cooking time, otherwise they might overcook.

• To prevent milk, cream or sour cream from curdling, add near the end of the cooking time and just heat through.

• Coating pot roasts and stew meat with flour helps to thicken the broth as it cooks. You can reduce the amount of liquid in the cooker by removing the lid and cooking on high for the last 15 to 20 minutes.

• When converting your favorite recipes for the slow cooker, reduce the amount of liquid since the slow cooker lid gives a tight seal and retains the steam. Pour the liquid in last, usually at least 1 cup. Fill the cooker at least one-half full of food for best results.

TIMING A SLOW COOKER

• Resist the urge to lift the lid and take a peek! The heat that you lose will add as much as 30 minutes to the cooking time. If you must stir, resume timing when the mixture begins to bubble again.

• Cooking for 1 hour on high is the same as 2 to 2½ hours on low.

• If food is not done within the time stated in the recipe, it could be because you live at an altitude above 4,000 feet, the voltage is low in your area, you have used frozen foods which take longer to heat, or you have filled your slow cooker too full.

• At altitudes above 4,000 feet, plan to cook your food for the maximum time specified in the recipe, especially if the recipe includes vegetables such as carrots, onion, celery, cabbage or potatoes or less tender cuts of meat such as brisket or pot roasts. Slow cooking at the low setting is better for tenderizing these cuts of meat than the high setting. Dried beans will tenderize best if soaked overnight (see page 54 for a suggested technique).

• After the food has finished cooking, it can usually be held in the slow cooker for an hour on the low setting without overcooking. If the food was originally cooked on the high setting, reduce the heat to low once it is done. Do check occasionally to see if it needs stirring or is overcooking.

REMOVAL OF EXCESS FAT

- Take time to trim and remove excess fat from your meat before cooking to reduce the amount of fat that accumulates during cooking.

- Before serving a cooked stew or soup (or thickening the liquid), skim off excess fat with a slice of bread (then give the bread to the dog!). Other methods of removing fat are to skim the surface with a lettuce leaf and discard, even celery leaves will work! OR, add a few ice cubes to the top to chill and congeal some of the fat, then spoon off the fat *and* ice cubes.

TRANSPORTING FOOD IN A SLOW COOKER

- If you are not cooking the food in a slow cooker, but want to transport and serve in one, preheat the container before adding the hot food by setting the empty slow cooker on low until warm.

- Use rubber bands to fasten the lid to the handles by wrapping the rubber bands around the knob on the lid and stretching them over the handles on the side of the cooker. If the rubber bands are too long to make the lid secure, double them or tie a knot in one end to shorten.

- Slow cookers can tip over if sitting on the floor of your car while driving! Place the slow cooker in a cardboard carton that is just slightly larger than the cooker. Fill in the space around the cooker with newspapers so the cooker will fit snugly in the carton. This will also act as insulation.

SLOW COOKER SAFETY

- Slow cookers generally have a relatively short cord to help prevent tangles and potential accidents. If you must use an extension cord, be sure the electrical rating is great enough to accommodate the needs of the appliance. If the cord gets warm or hot during use, it should not be used. Place the cooker on a sturdy, level surface where it will not be tipped over. Be sure the cord is out of the flow of traffic and does not touch the outside of the hot cooker.

- If preparing vegetables and browning meat the night before, cover the food and refrigerate. Place food in the slow cooker in the morning. Do not refrigerate the food in the slow cooker liner, since a cold slow cooker liner with cold food takes too long to heat and start cooking. Thus, the food may be in the "danger zone" longer than is recommended, causing spoilage and bacteria growth.

Pictured on following page: Chicken Eleganté (see page 27).

CREAMY HAM AND BROCCOLI

Makes 4 to 6 servings

Preparation Time: 10 minutes
Slow Cooker Cooking Time: 2 to 2½ hours on high or 4 to 5 hours on low
Last-Minute Cooking Time: none

> 1 pound cubed cooked ham (about 3 cups)
> 1 package (16 oz.) frozen cut broccoli,
>   thawed and drained
> 1 can (10¾ oz.) condensed cream of mushroom soup
> 1 jar (8 oz.) pasteurized process cheese spread
> 1 can (8 oz.) sliced water chestnuts, drained
> 1 cup uncooked instant rice
> 1 cup milk
> ½ cup chopped celery
> ½ cup chopped onion
> ⅛ to ¼ teaspoon pepper
>   Paprika (optional)

1. If desired, coat inside of a slow cooker with non-stick spray. In slow cooker, place ham, broccoli, soup, cheese spread, water chestnuts, rice, milk, celery, onion and pepper. Stir until blended. Smooth top, pushing rice into mixture.

2. Cover and cook on high for 2 to 2½ hours or on low for 4 to 5 hours or until rice and onion are tender, stirring occasionally if possible.

3. If desired, sprinkle with paprika before serving.

Serve with sliced beets or tomatoes and a relish plate.

NOTE: Mixture retains its heat and makes a great potluck dish.

High setting
2 to 2½ hours

Low setting
4 to 5 hours

Pictured on preceding page: Alpine Chicken (see page 17).

EASY CHICKEN A LA KING

Makes 4 servings

Preparation Time: 15 minutes
Slow Cooker Cooking Time: 2½ hours on high or 5 to 5½ hours on low
Last-Minute Cooking Time: 20 to 30 minutes on high

- 1½ **pounds boneless chicken breasts, skin removed**
- 1 **can (10¾ oz.) condensed cream of chicken or**
  cream of mushroom soup
- 3 **tablespoons all-purpose flour**
- ¼ **teaspoon pepper**
- 1 **package (10 oz.) frozen peas and onions,**
  thawed and well drained
- 2 **tablespoons chopped pimiento, drained**
- ½ **teaspoon paprika**
- ½ **teaspoon celery salt (optional)**
  Dash of cayenne pepper

1. Cut chicken into bite-size pieces. Place in a slow cooker.

2. In a medium bowl, stir soup, flour and pepper until blended. Pour over chicken. DO NOT STIR.

3. Cover and cook on high for 2½ hours or on low for 5 to 5½ hours or until chicken is very tender.

4. Stir in peas and onions, pimiento, paprika, celery salt if desired, and cayenne pepper. Cover and cook on high for 20 to 30 minutes or until vegetables are tender.

Serve over rice or in patty shells. Serve with fresh fruit.

High setting		Low setting
2½ hours		5 to 5½ hours

SPANISH CHICKEN AND RICE

Makes 4 to 6 servings

Preparation Time: 25 minutes
Slow Cooker Cooking Time: 2½ to 3 hours on high or 5 to 6 hours on low
Last-Minute Cooking Time: none

   1 to 1¼ pounds boneless chicken breasts,
      skin removed
  ¼ cup all-purpose flour
  ¼ teaspoon salt
  ⅛ teaspoon pepper
  ¼ pound bulk Italian sausage
  2 to 3 tablespoons vegetable oil
  3 medium tomatoes, peeled, cut up and juice reserved
  1 can (6 oz.) tomato juice (about ¾ cup)
  ¾ cup uncooked converted long grain rice
  ½ cup water
  1 teaspoon chicken bouillon granules
  ½ teaspoon dried Italian herb seasoning, crushed
  ½ cup chopped onion
  ½ cup diced green pepper
  1 large clove garlic, minced

1. If desired, coat inside of a slow cooker with non-stick spray. Cut chicken into ¾-inch pieces. In a plastic bag, mix flour, salt and pepper. Add chicken and shake until chicken is well coated; set aside.

2. In a medium skillet, crumble sausage. Over medium heat, brown sausage. Remove sausage and drain on paper towels. Place in slow cooker. Discard drippings.

3. In same skillet over medium-high heat, brown chicken in oil. Transfer chicken to slow cooker.

4. Place tomatoes with liquid, tomato juice, rice, water, bouillon granules and Italian seasoning in skillet. Stirring over medium heat, bring to a boil, loosening browned bits from bottom of skillet. Pour over chicken. Top with onion, green pepper and garlic and stir.

5. Cover and cook on high for 2½ to 3 hours or on low for 5 to 6 hours or until rice, vegetables and chicken are very tender.

6. Stir before serving.

Serve with steamed broccoli or buttered peas.

High setting
2½ to 3 hours

Low setting
5 to 6 hours

ITALIAN MEAT LOAF

Makes 8 servings

Preparation Time: 10 minutes
Slow Cooker Cooking Time: 2½ to 3 hours on high or 5 to 6 hours on low
Last-Minute Cooking Time: none

> 2 **pounds lean ground beef**
> 2 **cups soft bread crumbs**
> ½ **cup spaghetti sauce**
> 1 **large egg**
> 2 **tablespoons dried chopped onion**
> 1¼ **teaspoons salt**
> 1 **teaspoon garlic salt**
> ½ **teaspoon dried Italian herbs, crushed**
> ¼ **teaspoon garlic powder**
> ¼ **teaspoon pepper**
> 2 **tablespoons spaghetti sauce**

1. Fold a 30-inch long piece of foil in half lengthwise. Place in bottom of a slow cooker with both ends hanging over top edge of cooker.

2. In a large bowl, mix ground beef, bread crumbs, ½ cup spaghetti sauce, egg, onion, salt, garlic salt, Italian herbs, garlic powder and pepper until well blended. Shape into a loaf. Place in slow cooker on top of foil. Spread 2 tablespoons spaghetti sauce over top.

3. Cover tightly and cook on high for 2½ to 3 hours or on low for 5 to 6 hours or until beginning to brown and juices run clear.

4. Use ends of foil to lift out meat loaf and transfer to a serving platter.

Serve with spaghetti, any remaining spaghetti sauce and a spinach salad. Or chill, then slice and use for sandwiches.

High setting		**Low setting**
2½ to 3 hours		**5 to 6 hours**

CHICKEN MARENGO

Makes 4 to 6 servings

Preparation Time: 20 minutes
Slow Cooker Cooking Time: 2½ to 3 hours on high or 5 to 7 hours on low
Last-Minute Cooking Time: none

    8 **pieces chicken**
   ¼ **cup all-purpose flour**
    2 **tablespoons vegetable oil**
 1½ **cups frozen small white onions, partially thawed**
    1 **can (14½ oz.) stewed tomatoes, cut up and**
        juice reserved
    1 **can (4 oz.) sliced mushrooms, drained**
    1 **tablespoon dried parsley flakes, crushed**
    1 **bay leaf, broken in half**
    3 **or 4 cloves garlic, minced**
    1 **teaspoon salt**
   ½ **teaspoon dried thyme leaves, crushed**
   ¼ **teaspoon pepper**

1. Remove skin and excess fat from chicken; rinse and pat dry. Dip chicken in flour, shaking off excess; reserve remaining flour.

2. In a large skillet over medium-high heat, brown chicken in oil. Transfer chicken to a slow cooker, placing dark meat on bottom.

3. Place onions in skillet. Over medium-high heat, sauté for 2 minutes. Add stewed tomatoes with juice, mushrooms, parsley, bay leaf, garlic, salt, thyme, pepper and remaining flour. Stirring, bring to a boil, loosening browned bits from bottom of skillet. Pour over chicken.

4. Cover and cook on high for 2½ to 3 hours or on low for 5 to 7 hours or until chicken is very tender. Remove bay leaf.

Serve with spaghetti.

      High setting   **Low setting**
      2½ to 3 hours   **5 to 7 hours**

COMPANY CHICKEN AND MUSHROOMS

Makes 6 servings

Preparation Time: 15 minutes
Slow Cooker Cooking Time: 2½ to 3 hours on high or 5 to 6 hours on low
Last-Minute Cooking Time: about 5 minutes on stovetop

6	chicken breast halves (about 3¾ lb. total)
1¼	teaspoons salt
¼	teaspoon pepper
¼	teaspoon paprika
1¾	teaspoons chicken bouillon granules
1½	cups sliced mushrooms
½	cup sliced green onions
½	cup dry white wine or vermouth
1	can (5 oz.) evaporated milk
5	teaspoons cornstarch
	Minced fresh parsley

1. Remove skin from chicken; rinse and pat dry.

2. In a small bowl, mix salt, pepper and paprika. Rub into surface of chicken, using all of the mixture.

3. In a slow cooker, alternate layers of chicken, bouillon granules, mushrooms and green onions. Pour wine slowly over top. DO NOT STIR.

4. Cover and cook on high for 2½ to 3 hours or on low for 5 to 6 hours or until chicken is tender, but not falling off bone, basting once if time allows.

5. With a slotted spoon, remove chicken and vegetables to a serving platter. Cover with foil and keep warm.

6. In a small saucepan, stir evaporated milk and cornstarch until smooth. Gradually stir in 2 cups of the cooking liquid. Stirring over medium heat, bring to a boil and boil for 1 to 2 minutes or until thickened.

7. Spoon some of the sauce over chicken and garnish with parsley. Serve remaining sauce separately.

Serve with steamed rice.

High setting	Low setting
2½ to 3 hours	5 to 6 hours

POACHED CHICKEN AND BROTH

Makes about 4¼ cups chicken and about 3 cups broth

Preparation Time: 20 minutes
Slow Cooker Cooking Time: 2½ to 3 hours on high or 5 to 6 hours on low
Last-Minute Cooking Time: none
Cooling Time: 15 minutes or 1 hour

    3 **pounds chicken breast halves**
    2 **medium carrots, thinly sliced**
    3 **ribs celery, sliced**
    1 **medium onion, chopped**
    ½ **cup chopped fresh parsley**
    2 **teaspoons chicken bouillon granules**
    ¼ **teaspoon salt**
    ¼ **teaspoon pepper**
    3 **cups water**

1. Remove skin and excess fat from chicken; set aside.

2. Layer in a slow cooker, in order, carrots, celery, onion, chicken, parsley, bouillon granules, salt and pepper. Add water. DO NOT STIR.

3. Cover and cook on high for 2½ to 3 hours or on low for 5 to 6 hours or until chicken is tender.

4. If time allows, uncover and cool chicken in broth at room temperature, about 1 hour. Otherwise, when chicken is cool enough to handle, about 15 minutes, remove chicken from bones and cut or shred meat according to recipe use. Discard bones. Cooked chicken can be refrigerated up to 2 days before using.

5. Strain broth and discard vegetables. Refrigerate broth for another use, up to 2 days. Remove excess fat before using.

NOTE: For faster cooling, chicken can be removed from broth, but meat will be less moist.

High setting   **Low setting**
2½ to 3 hours   **5 to 6 hours**

LEMON GARLIC CHICKEN

Makes 4 servings

Preparation Time: 20 minutes
Slow Cooker Cooking Time: 2½ to 3 hours on high or 5 to 6 hours on low
Last-Minute Cooking Time: 15 to 30 minutes on high

- 2 **pounds chicken breast halves**
- 1 **teaspoon dried oregano leaves, crushed**
- ½ **teaspoon seasoned salt**
- ¼ **teaspoon pepper**
- 2 **tablespoons butter or margarine** ·
- ¼ **cup water**
- 3 **tablespoons lemon juice**
- 2 **cloves garlic, minced**
- 1 **teaspoon chicken bouillon granules**
- 1 **teaspoon minced fresh parsley**

1. Remove skin and excess fat from chicken; rinse and pat dry.

2. In a small bowl, mix oregano, seasoned salt and pepper; rub into chicken, using all of the mixture.

3. In a large skillet over medium heat, brown chicken in butter. Transfer chicken to a slow cooker.

4. Place water, lemon juice, garlic and bouillon granules in skillet. Stirring over medium heat, bring to a boil, loosening browned bits from bottom of skillet. Pour over chicken.

5. Cover and cook on high for 2½ to 3 hours or on low for 5 to 6 hours or until chicken is almost tender.

6. Add parsley and baste chicken. Cover and cook on high for 15 to 30 minutes or until chicken is tender and juices from chicken run clear when cut along bone in thickest portion.

Serve with rice pilaf.

High setting   **Low setting**
2½ to 3 hours   **5 to 6 hours**

TANGY FLANK STEAK

Makes 4 to 6 servings

Preparation Time: 10 minutes
Slow Cooker Cooking Time: 3 to 3½ hours on high or 6 to 7 hours on low
Last-Minute Cooking Time: none

    1 **beef flank steak (about 1½ lb.)**
    1 **to 2 tablespoons vegetable oil**
    1 **large onion, quartered and sliced**
    1 **can (4 oz.) chopped green chilies (optional), drained**
  ⅓ **cup water**
    2 **tablespoons vinegar**
 1¼ **teaspoons chili powder**
    1 **teaspoon garlic powder**
  ½ **teaspoon sugar**
  ½ **teaspoon salt**
  ⅛ **teaspoon pepper**

1. Cut flank steak in half if needed to fit in a slow cooker. In a large skillet over medium-high heat, brown flank steak in oil. Place in slow cooker.

2. In skillet, place onion, green chilies if desired, water, vinegar, chili powder, garlic powder, sugar, salt and pepper. Bring to a boil over medium heat, stirring to loosen browned bits from bottom of skillet. Pour over meat.

3. Cover and cook on high for 3 to 3½ hours or on low for 6 to 7 hours or until meat is very tender.

4. Transfer meat to a warm platter. Slice meat diagonally. Remove onion from slow cooker with a slotted spoon and arrange around meat. If desired, baste with juices.

Serve with baked potatoes and sour cream.

High setting
3 to 3½ hours

Low setting
6 to 7 hours

POLISH KRAUT 'N' APPLES

(pictured on page 43)

Makes 4 servings

Preparation Time: 10 minutes
Slow Cooker Cooking Time: 3 to 3½ hours on high or 6 to 7 hours on low
Last-Minute Cooking Time: none

- 1 **pound fresh or canned sauerkraut**
- 1 **pound lean smoked Polish sausage**
- 3 **tart cooking apples, thickly sliced (peel if desired)**
- ½ **cup packed brown sugar**
- ¾ **teaspoon salt**
- ⅛ **teaspoon pepper**
- ½ **teaspoon caraway seeds (optional)**
- ¾ **cup apple juice or cider**

1. Rinse sauerkraut and squeeze dry. Place half of the sauerkraut in a slow cooker.

2. Cut sausage into 2-inch lengths. Place in slow cooker.

3. Continue to layer in slow cooker, in order, apples, brown sugar, salt, pepper and, if desired, caraway seeds. Top with remaining sauerkraut. Add apple juice. DO NOT STIR.

4. Cover and cook on high for 3 to 3½ hours or on low for 6 to 7 hours or until apples are tender.

5. Stir before serving.

Serve with small boiled potatoes and French or rye bread.

High setting   **Low setting**
3 to 3½ hours   **6 to 7 hours**

ALPINE CHICKEN

(pictured on page 6)

Makes 4 to 6 servings

Preparation Time: 15 to 20 minutes
Slow Cooker Cooking Time: 3 to 3½ hours on high or 6 to 8 hours on low
Last-Minute Cooking Time: 6 to 8 minutes under broiler

> 2 **teaspoons chicken bouillon granules**
> 1 **tablespoon chopped fresh parsley**
> ¾ **teaspoon poultry seasoning**
> ⅓ **cup diced Canadian bacon**
> 2 to 3 **carrots, thinly sliced**
> 1 to 2 **ribs celery, thinly sliced**
> 1 **small onion, thinly sliced**
> ¼ **cup water**
> 1 **broiler-fryer chicken (about 3 lb.), cut up**
> 1 **can (11 oz.) condensed Cheddar cheese soup**
> 1 **tablespoon all-purpose flour**
> 1 **package (16 oz.) wide egg noodles, cooked and**
>   **drained**
> 2 **tablespoons sliced pimiento**
> 2 **tablespoons grated Parmesan cheese**

1. In a small bowl, mix bouillon granules, chopped parsley and poultry seasoning; set aside.

2. Layer in a slow cooker, in order, Canadian bacon, carrots, celery and onion. Add water.

3. Remove skin, if desired, and excess fat from chicken; rinse and pat dry. Place white meat in slow cooker. Sprinkle with half of the reserved seasoning mixture. Top with remaining chicken and sprinkle with remaining seasoning mixture. Stir soup and flour together, spoon over top. DO NOT STIR.

4. Cover and cook on high for 3 to 3½ hours or on low for 6 to 8 hours or until chicken is tender and juices from chicken run clear when cut along the bone and vegetables are tender.

5. Spread cooked noodles in a shallow 2- or 2½-quart broiler-proof serving dish. Arrange chicken on noodles. Stir soup mixture and vegetables until combined. Spoon vegetables and some of the liquid over chicken. Sprinkle with pimiento and Parmesan cheese.

6. Broil 6 inches from heat source for 6 to 8 minutes or until lightly browned. Garnish with parsley sprig if desired.

Serve with mixed green salad and hard rolls.

High setting
3 to 3½ hours

Low setting
6 to 8 hours

FRUITED CARIBBEAN CHOPS

Makes 6 servings

Preparation Time: 20 minutes
Slow Cooker Cooking Time: 3 to 3½ hours on high or 6 to 7 hours on low
Last-Minute Cooking Time: 10 minutes on high

6 pork loin chops (about 2 lb. total)
3 tablespoons all-purpose flour
1½ teaspoons dried oregano leaves, crushed
1½ teaspoons salt
¼ teaspoon pepper
¼ teaspoon garlic powder
2 tablespoons vegetable oil
1 can (15¼ oz.) pineapple chunks in own juice
1 can (6 oz.) pineapple juice (¾ cup)
¼ cup water
2 tablespoons brown sugar
2 tablespoons dried chopped onion
2 tablespoons tomato paste
¼ cup raisins

1. Trim excess fat from chops. On a sheet of waxed paper or in a shallow dish, mix flour, oregano, salt, pepper and garlic powder until uniform. Rub flour mixture on both sides of chops until well coated, using all the mixture.

2. In a 10-inch skillet over medium-high heat, brown 2 or 3 chops at a time in oil; transfer to a slow cooker.

3. Drain pineapple juice from pineapple into a small bowl; set chunks aside. To small bowl, add ¾ cup pineapple juice, water, brown sugar, onion and tomato paste; stir until well blended. Pour mixture into slow cooker. Sprinkle raisins on top.

4. Cover and cook on high for 3 to 3½ hours or on low for 6 to 7 hours or until meat is tender.

5. Skim off fat from liquid in slow cooker. Stir pineapple chunks into mixture and cook on high for 10 minutes or until heated through.

Serve with brown rice and steamed asparagus spears.

High setting
3 to 3½ hours

Low setting
6 to 7 hours

STEAK STROGANOFF

Makes 6 servings

Preparation Time: 15 minutes
Slow Cooker Cooking Time: 3 to 3½ hours on high or 6 to 7 hours on low
Last-Minute Cooking Time: 10 to 15 minutes on high

- 2 **tablespoons all-purpose flour**
- ½ **teaspoon garlic powder**
- ½ **teaspoon pepper**
- ¼ **teaspoon paprika**
- 1 **boneless beef round steak (about 1¾ lb.)**
- 1 **can (10¾ oz.) condensed cream of mushroom soup**
- ½ **cup water**
- 1 **package (1 oz.) dried onion mushroom soup mix**
- 1 **jar (9 oz.) sliced mushrooms, drained**
- ½ **cup dairy sour cream**
- 1 **tablespoon minced fresh parsley**

1. In a slow cooker, combine flour, garlic powder, pepper and paprika.

2. Trim excess fat from beef; cut meat into 1½ x ½-inch strips. Place in flour mixture and toss meat until well coated. Add mushroom soup, water and soup mix. Stir until blended.

3. Cover and cook on high for 3 to 3½ hours or on low for 6 to 7 hours or until meat is very tender.

4. Stir in mushrooms, sour cream and parsley. Immediately cover and cook on high for 10 to 15 minutes or until heated through.

Serve with beef-flavored rice and a spinach salad.

High setting
3 to 3½ hours

Low setting
6 to 7 hours

BROWN BEEF RAGOUT

Makes 6 to 8 servings

Preparation Time: 30 minutes
Slow Cooker Cooking Time: 3 to 4 hours on high or 6 to 8 hours on low
Last-Minute Cooking Time: none

> ½ cup all-purpose flour
> 1¼ teaspoons garlic salt
> ¼ teaspoon pepper
> 1 boneless beef chuck roast (about 2½ lb.),
>   cut in 1-inch pieces
> 3 to 6 tablespoons vegetable oil
> 1 package (10 oz.) frozen crinkle-cut carrots
> 1 package (16 oz.) frozen small whole onions
> ½ cup sliced celery
> 2 cans (4 oz. each) sliced mushrooms, drained
> 1 tablespoon dried parsley flakes, crushed
> ½ cup water
> 1 can (10¾ oz.) condensed cream of celery soup
> 1 cup dry red wine
> 2 teaspoons beef bouillon granules

1. In a plastic bag, mix flour, garlic salt and pepper. Add meat and shake until meat is evenly coated with all of the flour mixture.

2. In a large skillet over medium-high heat, brown half of the meat at a time in 3 tablespoons of the oil, using additional oil as needed; set aside.

3. Rinse frozen carrots and onions under hot running water to thaw slightly; drain well.

4. Layer in a slow cooker, in order, celery, meat, carrots, onions, mushrooms and parsley. DO NOT STIR.

5. Add water to skillet. Cook over medium-high heat, stirring to loosen browned bits from bottom of skillet. Add soup, wine and bouillon granules. Stir until blended. Pour over mixture in slow cooker.

6. Cover and cook on high for 3 to 4 hours or on low for 6 to 8 hours or until meat, celery and carrots are tender.

Serve with wide egg noodles.

High setting   **Low setting**
3 to 4 hours   **6 to 8 hours**

MAGGIE'S STEW

Makes 4 servings

Preparation Time: 20 minutes
Slow Cooker Cooking Time: 3 to 4 hours on high or 6 to 8 hours on low
Last-Minute Cooking Time: none

        4 **carrots, sliced**
        2 **medium turnips, cubed**
     1½ **cups frozen small white onions, thawed**
            (about ½ of a 16 oz. package)
      10 **medium mushrooms (optional), halved**
     1¼ **pounds lean lamb shoulder, cubed**
        1 **to 2 tablespoons vegetable oil**
       ¼ **cup all-purpose flour**
        1 **cup water**
        2 **tablespoons catsup or chili sauce**
        2 **teaspoons Worcestershire sauce**
        2 **teaspoons beef bouillon granules**
        2 **cloves garlic, minced**
       ¼ **teaspoon salt**
       ¼ **teaspoon pepper**
        2 **teaspoons dried parsley flakes, crushed**

1. In a slow cooker, place carrots, turnips, onions and, if desired, mushrooms.

2. In a large skillet over medium-high heat, lightly brown lamb in oil. Sprinkle with flour. Cook and stir until flour is lightly browned.

3. Add water, catsup, Worcestershire sauce, bouillon granules, garlic, salt and pepper. Cook over medium heat, stirring to loosen browned bits from bottom of skillet. Pour over vegetables in slow cooker. Stir until blended.

4. Cover and cook on high for 3 to 4 hours or on low for 6 to 8 hours or until meat and vegetables are very tender. Stir in parsley.

Serve with biscuits or cooked barley and a fruit salad.

High setting   **Low setting**
3 to 4 hours   **6 to 8 hours**

SPOONBURGERS

Makes 6 servings

Preparation Time: 10 minutes
Slow Cooker Cooking Time: 3 to 4 hours on high or 6 to 8 hours on low
Last-Minute Cooking Time: 5 to 10 minutes on stovetop

1½	**pounds extra lean ground beef**
1	**small green pepper, chopped**
1	**small onion, chopped**
½	**cup chopped fresh parsley**
1	**can (8 oz.) tomato sauce**
1	**can (8 oz.) stewed tomatoes, cut up and juice reserved**
1	**can (4 oz.) chopped green chilies**
1	**tablespoon chili powder**
1	**or 2 cloves garlic, minced**
1¼	**teaspoons salt**
½	**teaspoon paprika**
¼	**teaspoon pepper**
	Toasted split buns or cooked pasta

1. Crumble ground beef and place in a slow cooker. Add green pepper, onion, parsley, tomato sauce, stewed tomatoes with juice, green chilies, chili powder, garlic, salt, paprika and pepper. Stir well, scraping sides.

2. Cover and cook on high for 3 to 4 hours or on low for 6 to 8 hours or until vegetables are tender.

3. Spoon over buns or pasta.

Serve with French fries and pickles.

High setting
3 to 4 hours

Low setting
6 to 8 hours

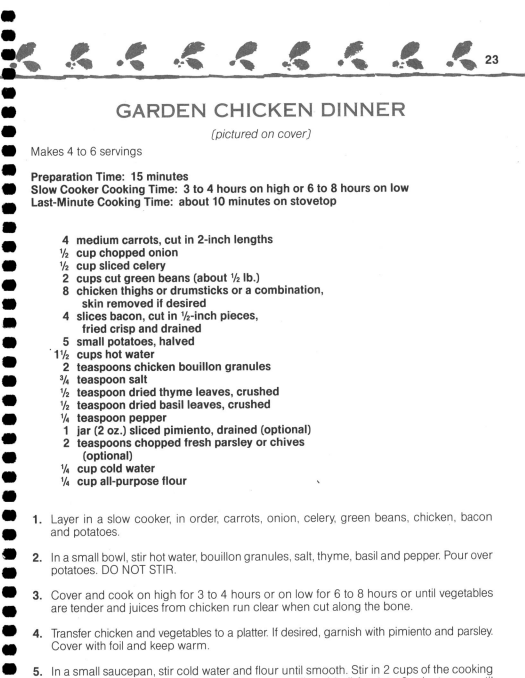

GARDEN CHICKEN DINNER

(pictured on cover)

Makes 4 to 6 servings

Preparation Time: 15 minutes
Slow Cooker Cooking Time: 3 to 4 hours on high or 6 to 8 hours on low
Last-Minute Cooking Time: about 10 minutes on stovetop

> 4 medium carrots, cut in 2-inch lengths
> ½ cup chopped onion
> ½ cup sliced celery
> 2 cups cut green beans (about ½ lb.)
> 8 chicken thighs or drumsticks or a combination,
>   skin removed if desired
> 4 slices bacon, cut in ½-inch pieces,
>   fried crisp and drained
> 5 small potatoes, halved
> 1½ cups hot water
> 2 teaspoons chicken bouillon granules
> ¾ teaspoon salt
> ½ teaspoon dried thyme leaves, crushed
> ½ teaspoon dried basil leaves, crushed
> ¼ teaspoon pepper
> 1 jar (2 oz.) sliced pimiento, drained (optional)
> 2 teaspoons chopped fresh parsley or chives
>   (optional)
> ¼ cup cold water
> ¼ cup all-purpose flour

1. Layer in a slow cooker, in order, carrots, onion, celery, green beans, chicken, bacon and potatoes.

2. In a small bowl, stir hot water, bouillon granules, salt, thyme, basil and pepper. Pour over potatoes. DO NOT STIR.

3. Cover and cook on high for 3 to 4 hours or on low for 6 to 8 hours or until vegetables are tender and juices from chicken run clear when cut along the bone.

4. Transfer chicken and vegetables to a platter. If desired, garnish with pimiento and parsley. Cover with foil and keep warm.

5. In a small saucepan, stir cold water and flour until smooth. Stir in 2 cups of the cooking liquid. Stirring over medium heat, bring to a boil and boil for 1 to 2 minutes or until thickened. Serve sauce separately.

Serve with croissants.

High setting 3 to 4 hours		**Low setting** 6 to 8 hours

MOM'S SUNDAY CHICKEN

Makes 4 to 6 servings

Preparation Time: 20 minutes
Slow Cooker Cooking Time: 3 to 4 hours on high or 6 to 8 hours on low
Last-Minute Cooking Time: about 10 minutes on stovetop

- 1 **broiler-fryer chicken (about 3 lb.), cut up**
- 2 **to 3 tablespoons vegetable oil**
- 6 **to 8 small potatoes, peeled and quartered**
- ½ **cup water**
- 2 **tablespoons dried parsley flakes, crushed**
- 1 **teaspoon chicken bouillon granules**
- 1 **teaspoon dried thyme leaves, crushed**
- 1 **teaspoon Dijon mustard**
- ½ **teaspoon salt**
- ⅛ **teaspoon pepper**
  Milk (about ¼ cup)
- 1 **package (about ⅞ oz.) mushroom sauce or**
  chicken gravy mix
  Chopped fresh parsley

1. Remove excess fat from chicken. In a large skillet over medium-high heat, brown chicken in oil. Transfer chicken to a slow cooker, placing dark meat on bottom. Place potatoes in slow cooker.

2. Discard any excess oil in skillet. Add water, dried parsley, bouillon granules, thyme, Dijon mustard, salt and pepper. Stirring, bring to a boil, loosening browned bits from bottom of skillet. Pour over chicken and potatoes.

3. Cover and cook on high for 3 to 4 hours or on low for 6 to 8 hours or until juices from chicken run clear and potatoes are tender.

4. Transfer chicken and potatoes to a warm serving platter. Cover and keep warm.

5. Skim fat from cooking liquid. Measure cooking liquid and add enough milk to equal 1¼ cups liquid or enough to equal amount of liquid on package directions.

6. In a small saucepan, stir liquid and sauce mix until blended. Stirring over medium heat, bring to a boil and boil until slightly thickened.

7. Sprinkle chicken and potatoes with fresh parsley. Serve sauce separately.

Serve with buttered green beans and tossed green salad.

High setting		Low setting
3 to 4 hours		6 to 8 hours

Pictured on following page: Chinese Beef and Tomatoes (see page 36).

CHICKEN ELEGANTÉ

(pictured on page 5)

Makes 4 to 6 servings

Preparation Time: 20 minutes
Slow Cooker Cooking Time: 3 to 4 hours on high or 6 to 8 hours on low
Last-Minute Cooking Time: 15 minutes on high plus about 5 minutes on stovetop

    1 **broiler-fryer chicken (about 4 lb.), cut up**
    2 **tablespoons butter or margarine**
    1 **can (6 oz.) frozen orange juice concentrate, thawed**
    2 **teaspoons chicken bouillon granules**
    1 **teaspoon celery salt**
  ¾ **teaspoon lemon-pepper seasoning**
  ¼ **teaspoon ground allspice**
  ¼ **teaspoon ground cinnamon**
    1 **can (16 oz.) sliced peaches, drained**
  ¾ **cup seedless grapes**
    3 **tablespoons cold water**
2½ **tablespoons cornstarch**
  ¼ **cup toasted sliced almonds (optional)**

1. Remove skin, if desired, and excess fat from chicken pieces; rinse and pat dry. In a large skillet over medium-low heat, brown chicken in butter. Do not crowd pieces.

2. Meanwhile, in a small bowl, stir orange juice concentrate, bouillon granules, celery salt, ½ teaspoon of the lemon-pepper seasoning, allspice and cinnamon until blended.

3. Place several pieces of chicken in a slow cooker. Spoon some of the orange mixture over chicken to coat. Repeat with remaining chicken and orange mixture.

4. Cover and cook on high for 3 to 4 hours or on low for 6 to 8 hours or until chicken is tender, but not falling off bone. Baste while cooking if desired, replacing lid quickly.

5. Gently stir in peaches and grapes. Cover and heat for 15 minutes.

6. With a slotted spoon, remove chicken and fruit to a warm serving platter. Cover tightly with foil and keep warm.

7. In a small saucepan, stir water and cornstarch until smooth. Gradually stir in 2 cups cooking liquid and remaining ¼ teaspoon lemon-pepper seasoning. Stirring over medium heat, bring to a boil and boil for 1 to 2 minutes or until thickened.

8. Spoon some of the sauce over chicken; garnish with almonds. Serve sauce separately.

Serve with wild rice and steamed broccoli spears.

High setting
3 to 4 hours

Low setting
6 to 8 hours

Pictured on preceding page: Farmer's-style chops (see page 33) and Italian Vegetable Soup (see page 40).

OLD-FASHIONED TURKEY SOUP

Makes 6 (1½-cup) servings

Preparation Time: 20 minutes
Slow Cooker Cooking Time: 3 to 4 hours on high or 6 to 8 hours on low
Last-Minute Cooking Time: 25 minutes on high

1	cup diced carrots
½	cup chopped onion
1	cup sliced celery
1	cup cut green beans, fresh if available
1	cup shredded cabbage
1	cup sliced mushrooms
2	turkey thighs (about 2¼ lb. total)
5	cups warm water
3	teaspoons chicken bouillon granules
2	teaspoons bottled steak sauce
1	teaspoon dried thyme leaves, crushed
½	teaspoon salt
⅛	teaspoon pepper
⅔	cup uncooked instant rice

1. In a slow cooker, layer in order, carrots, onion, celery, green beans, cabbage and mushrooms.

2. Remove skin and excess fat from turkey. Place thighs in slow cooker.

3. Add water, bouillon granules, steak sauce, thyme, salt and pepper.

4. Cover and cook on high for 3 to 4 hours or on low for 6 to 8 hours or until turkey, carrots and green beans are tender when pierced with a fork.

5. Remove turkey from mixture to cool. Quickly stir rice into soup. Cover and cook on high for 15 minutes or until rice is done.

6. Meanwhile, when turkey is cool enough to handle, remove turkey from bone and cut into bite-size pieces. Discard bones. Return turkey to soup. Cover and cook on high 10 minutes longer or until heated through. Taste for seasoning and add additional salt if needed.

Serve with hot garlic bread.

High setting		Low setting
3 to 4 hours		6 to 8 hours

HERBED SWISS STEAK

Makes 6 servings

Preparation Time: 25 minutes
Slow Cooker Cooking Time: 3½ to 4 hours on high or 7 to 8 hours on low
Last-Minute Cooking Time: none

> 1 **boneless beef round steak (about 1½ lb.)**
> 1 **teaspoon dry mustard**
> ½ **cup all-purpose flour**
> 2 **slices bacon, cut in 1-inch pieces**
> 1 **to 3 tablespoons vegetable oil**
> ½ **teaspoon salt**
> ½ **teaspoon dried rosemary leaves, crushed**
> ½ **teaspoon dried thyme leaves, crushed**
> 1 **cup frozen small white onions**
> 1¾ **cups water**
> 1½ **cups tomato juice**
> 2 **cloves garlic, minced**

1. Trim excess fat from steak. Cut meat into six serving pieces. Rub pieces with dry mustard. Dip in flour. Pound with a meat mallet until as much flour as possible sticks to meat. Reserve any remaining flour. Set meat aside.

2. In a large skillet over medium heat, brown bacon until crisp. Remove bacon and drain on paper towels.

3. Add 1 tablespoon of the oil to bacon drippings in skillet. Brown meat in oil, adding additional oil if needed.

4. In a small bowl, mix salt, rosemary and thyme. Sprinkle mixture on each piece of meat. Place meat in a slow cooker.

5. Using same skillet over medium heat, brown onions. Transfer onions to slow cooker. Pour off excess drippings.

6. Stir reserved flour into drippings in skillet until lightly browned. Stir in water, tomato juice and garlic. Stirring, bring to a boil; pour over meat and onions. Sprinkle with reserved bacon pieces.

7. Cover and cook on high for 3½ to 4 hours or on low for 7 to 8 hours or until meat is very tender.

8. Transfer meat to a serving platter. Serve with sauce.

Serve with mashed potatoes and Waldorf salad.

High setting   **Low setting**
3½ to 4 hours   **7 to 8 hours**

GOOD OL' CHILI

Makes 6 to 8 servings

Preparation Time: 10 minutes
Slow Cooker Cooking Time: 3½ to 4 hours on high or 7 to 8 hours on low
Last-Minute Cooking Time: none

1½	pounds extra lean ground beef
2	or 3 cans (15 oz. each) pinto beans, drained
1	large onion, chopped
3	large cloves garlic, minced
1	can (15 oz.) whole tomatoes, cut up and juice reserved
1	can (6 oz.) tomato paste
½	cup water
2	to 3 tablespoons chili powder
2	teaspoons salt
1	teaspoon dried oregano leaves, crushed
1	teaspoon ground cumin
¼	teaspoon pepper

1. Crumble ground beef into a slow cooker. Add beans, onion and garlic.

2. In a medium bowl, stir tomatoes with juice, tomato paste, water, chili powder, salt, oregano, cumin and pepper until blended. Stir into meat mixture. Scrape down sides of slow cooker.

3. Cover and cook on high for 3½ to 4 hours or on low for 7 to 8 hours or until onion is tender.

Serve with shredded Cheddar cheese and saltine crackers or tortilla chips.

High setting	**Low setting**
3½ to 4 hours	**7 to 8 hours**

HEARTY CASSOULET

Makes 6 servings

Preparation Time: 15 minutes
Slow Cooker Cooking Time: 3½ to 4 hours on high or 7 to 8 hours on low
Last-Minute Cooking Time: none

　　1　**large onion, chopped**
　　3　**small carrots, thinly sliced**
　　3　**cloves garlic, minced**
　　3　**cans (15 oz. each) Great Northern white beans**
　　3　**teaspoons chicken bouillon granules**
　　1　**tablespoon tomato paste**
　　1　**medium bay leaf**
　　1　**teaspoon dried thyme leaves, crushed**
　¼　**teaspoon pepper**
　1½　**pounds chicken thighs or pork loin chops, cut in half**
　　1　**pound smoked garlic sausage links,**
　　　　cut in 2-inch pieces
　¼　**pound bacon, cut in 1-inch pieces**

1. Layer in a slow cooker, in order, onion, carrots, garlic, beans with liquid, bouillon granules, tomato paste, bay leaf, thyme, pepper, chicken or pork, sausage and bacon. DO NOT STIR.

2. Cover and cook on high for 3½ to 4 hours or on low for 7 to 8 hours or until vegetables and meat are tender. Remove bay leaf.

Serve with broiled tomatoes, hot French bread and sweet pickles.

High setting
3½ to 4 hours

Low setting
7 to 8 hours

TONY'S CHUNKY SPAGHETTI SAUCE

Makes about 6 cups

Preparation Time: 20 minutes
Slow Cooker Cooking Time: 3½ to 4 hours on high or 7 to 8 hours on low
Last-Minute Cooking Time: none

- 1 **pound lean ground beef**
- ½ **pound bulk mild pork sausage**
- 1 **can (28 oz.) Italian tomatoes with basil, cut up and**
  juice reserved
- 1 **can (6 oz.) tomato paste**
- 1 **medium onion, finely chopped**
- ¾ **cup dry red wine or water**
- 2 **tablespoons chopped parsley**
- 2 **teaspoons sugar**
- 1 **teaspoon dried basil leaves, crushed**
- 1 **teaspoon salt**
- ¼ **teaspoon garlic powder**
- ⅛ **teaspoon pepper**

1. In a large skillet, coarsely crumble ground beef and sausage. Over medium heat, cook until browned. Drain on paper towels.

2. In a slow cooker, place cooked meat, tomatoes with juice, tomato paste, onion, wine, parsley, sugar, basil, salt, garlic powder and pepper. Stir until combined.

3. Cover and cook on high for 3½ to 4 hours or on low for 7 to 8 hours or until onion is tender.

Serve over spaghetti with grated Parmesan cheese. Serve with a romaine salad.

High setting   **Low setting**
3½ to 4 hours   **7 to 8 hours**

FARMER'S-STYLE CHOPS

(pictured on page 26)

Makes 6 servings

Preparation Time: 20 minutes
Slow Cooker Cooking Time: 3½ to 4 hours on high or 7 to 8 hours on low
Last-Minute Cooking Time: about 5 minutes on stovetop

- 6 pork loin chops
- 4 tablespoons all-purpose flour
- 2 tablespoons vegetable oil
- 3 medium potatoes, cubed
- 1 medium onion, chopped
- 1 small cabbage, cut in thin wedges
- ¼ teaspoon salt
- ½ teaspoon pepper
- 2 teaspoons beef bouillon granules
- ¼ cup water
- 1 can (14½ oz.) stewed tomatoes,
     cut up and juice reserved
- ½ cup dairy sour cream
- 2 tablespoons cornstarch
     Water or milk
     Chopped chives or parsley (optional)

1. Trim excess fat from chops. Coat chops with 2 tablespoons of the flour. In a large skillet over medium heat, brown chops in oil.

2. In a slow cooker, place potatoes and onion. Sprinkle remaining flour over and toss to coat. Layer over potato mixture, in order, cabbage, salt, pepper, pork chops, bouillon granules, ¼ cup water and stewed tomatoes with juice. DO NOT STIR.

3. Cover and cook on high for 3½ to 4 hours or on low for 7 to 8 hours or until vegetables and pork chops are tender.

4. To serve, transfer meat and vegetables to a large platter; cover and keep warm.

5. In a small saucepan, stir sour cream and cornstarch until smooth. Measure cooking liquid and add enough water or milk to equal 1½ cups. Stir into saucepan. Cook and stir over medium heat until thickened and mixture comes to a boil. Serve with chops. Garnish with chives if desired.

Serve with corn bread sticks and a cottage cheese-fruit salad.

High setting   **Low setting**
3½ to 4 hours   **7 to 8 hours**

CURRIED PORK

Makes 6 servings

Preparation Time: 15 minutes
Slow Cooker Cooking Time: 3½ to 4 hours on high or 7 to 8 hours on low
Last-Minute Cooking Time: 5 minutes on high

        3 **tablespoons all-purpose flour**
        2 **to 3 teaspoons curry powder**
       ¼ **teaspoon salt**
       ⅛ **teaspoon ground cloves**
     1½ **pounds lean pork stew meat**
        2 **tablespoons butter or margarine**
        1 **medium onion, chopped**
        3 **teaspoons beef bouillon granules**
        1 **or 2 cloves garlic, minced**
        3 **large tart cooking apples, diced**
        1 **can (8 oz.) tomato sauce**
       ½ **cup water**
       ¼ **cup raisins**
        1 **tablespoon lemon juice**

1. In a medium bowl, mix flour, curry powder, salt and cloves. Toss meat in mixture until well coated.

2. In a large skillet over medium heat, brown meat in butter. Place meat in a slow cooker.

3. Layer over meat, in order, onion, bouillon granules, garlic and apples. Pour tomato sauce and water over apples. DO NOT STIR.

4. Cover and cook on high for 3½ to 4 hours or on low for 7 to 8 hours or until meat is very tender.

5. Stir in raisins and lemon juice. Cover and cook on high for 5 minutes or until raisins are softened.

Serve with couscous or hot cooked rice, sliced green onions, toasted coconut and chopped peanuts.

NOTE: Other lean stew meats such as beef or lamb can be used or a combination.

High setting
3½ to 4 hours

Low setting
7 to 8 hours

TERIYAKI PORK ROAST

Makes 8 servings

Preparation Time: 10 minutes
Slow Cooker Cooking Time: 3½ to 4 hours on high or 7 to 8 hours on low
Last-Minute Cooking Time: about 5 minutes on stovetop

> 1 **can (6 oz.) apple juice (¾ cup)**
> 2 **tablespoons sugar**
> 2 **tablespoons soy sauce**
> 1 **tablespoon vinegar**
> 1 **teaspoon ground ginger**
> ¼ **teaspoon garlic powder**
> ⅛ **teaspoon pepper**
> 1 **lean boneless pork rolled loin roast (about 2¾ lb.)**
> 3 **tablespoons cold water**
> 1½ **tablespoons cornstarch**

1. In a slow cooker, mix apple juice, sugar, soy sauce, vinegar, ginger, garlic powder and pepper. Add roast, turning to coat. Turn fat-side up.

2. Cover and cook on high for 3½ to 4 hours or on low for 7 to 8 hours or until meat is very tender.

3. Transfer meat to a warm platter. Cover and keep warm.

4. Strain cooking liquid and place in a small saucepan (you will have about 1⅔ cups). Skim off fat if desired. Over medium heat, bring to a boil.

5. Meanwhile, in a small bowl, mix water and cornstarch until smooth. Stir into boiling liquid. Stirring, bring to a boil and boil for 1 to 2 minutes or until thickened. Serve sauce separately.

Serve with fried rice and mixed Oriental vegetables.

High setting
3½ to 4 hours

Low setting
7 to 8 hours

CHINESE BEEF AND TOMATOES

(pictured on page 25)

Makes 4 servings

Preparation Time: 15 minutes
Slow Cooker Cooking Time: 3½ to 4 hours on high or 7 to 8 hours on low
Last-Minute Cooking Time: 15 minutes on high

- 1 **medium onion, halved and sliced**
- 1 **small green pepper, coarsely chopped**
- 2 **ribs celery, sliced**
- 3 **tablespoons soy sauce**
- ¼ **teaspoon garlic powder**
- ¼ **teaspoon pepper**
- 1 **pound boneless beef round steak,**
     cut in 1½ x ⅛-inch strips
- 1 **tablespoon butter or margarine**
- ½ **cup water**
- 1 **teaspoon beef bouillon granules**
- 1 **tablespoon cold water**
- 1 **tablespoon cornstarch**
- 1½ **teaspoons sugar**
- ¼ **teaspoon ground ginger**
- 1 **pint cherry tomatoes, halved, or 2 large tomatoes,**
     each cut in 8 wedges

1. Place onion, green pepper and celery in a slow cooker.

2. In a pie plate, stir 2 tablespoons of the soy sauce, garlic powder and pepper. Add meat and stir until well coated.

3. In a large skillet over medium heat, brown meat in butter. Place meat in slow cooker.

4. To skillet, add ½ cup water and bouillon granules. Over medium heat, bring to a boil, stirring to loosen browned bits from bottom of skillet. Pour over meat. Stir once.

5. Cover and cook on high for 3½ to 4 hours or on low for 7 to 8 hours or until meat and onion are tender.

6. In a small bowl, stir remaining 1 tablespoon soy sauce, 1 tablespoon water, cornstarch, sugar and ginger until smooth. Stir into liquid in slow cooker. Stir in tomatoes.

7. Cover and cook on high for 15 minutes or until thickened and tomatoes are heated through.

Serve with Chinese egg noodles and additional soy sauce.

High setting   **Low setting**
3½ to 4 hours   **7 to 8 hours**

HAM-VEGETABLE SOUP

Makes 6 (1½-cup) servings

Preparation Time: 10 minutes
Slow Cooker Cooking Time: 3½ to 4 hours on high or 7 to 8 hours on low
Last-Minute Cooking Time: 20 to 30 minutes on high

> 1 **medium onion, chopped**
> 2 **cloves garlic, minced**
> 1 **pound sliced smoked ham hocks, cut in pieces**
> ½ **cup chopped green pepper**
> 2 **cans (15 oz. each) Great Northern white beans**
> 1 **can (8½ oz.) lima beans**
> ¼ **teaspoon hot pepper sauce**
> 1½ **teaspoons chicken bouillon granules**
> ½ **teaspoon dried thyme leaves, crushed**
> 1 **cup hot water**
> 1 **package (10 oz.) frozen peas and carrots,* thawed**
> 1 **cup thinly shredded cabbage (optional)**

1. Layer in a slow cooker, in order, onion, garlic, ham hocks, green pepper, beans with liquid, hot pepper sauce, bouillon granules, thyme and water. DO NOT STIR.

2. Cover and cook on high for 3½ to 4 hours or on low for 7 to 8 hours or until ham hocks are very tender.

3. Stir in thawed vegetables and cabbage. Immediately cover and cook on high for 20 to 30 minutes or until vegetables are tender and heated through.

Serve with green salad and corn muffins.

*Or use ½ package (20 oz.) frozen Italian or California-style vegetables, thawed.

High setting
3½ to 4 hours

Low setting
7 to 8 hours

SPANISH STEW

Makes 6 to 8 servings

Preparation Time: 30 minutes
Slow Cooker Cooking Time: 3½ to 4 hours on high or 7 to 8 hours on low
Last-Minute Cooking Time: 20 to 30 minutes on high

- 1 **boneless lean beef chuck roast (about 2¾ lb.)**
- ¼ **cup all-purpose flour**
- 1½ **teaspoons sugar**
- 2 to 3 **tablespoons vegetable oil**
- 3 **medium carrots, cut in 2-inch strips**
- 3 **ribs celery, cut in ½-inch pieces**
- 1 **can (3¼ oz.) pitted medium ripe olives, drained**
- 1 **medium onion, chopped**
- 2 to 3 **large cloves garlic, minced**
- 1 **can (14½ oz.) sliced stewed tomatoes**
- ½ **cup dry red wine or water**
- 2 **tablespoons tomato paste (optional)**
- 1 **teaspoon dried basil leaves**
- ½ **teaspoon dried thyme leaves**
- 1 **teaspoon salt**
- ¼ **teaspoon pepper**
- 2 **medium zucchini, cut in half lengthwise and sliced**
  (about 2 cups), or 1 cup frozen peas,
  thawed and drained

1. Trim excess fat from meat. Cut into 1½-inch pieces. Toss in a mixture of flour and sugar until coated.

2. In a large skillet over medium heat, brown meat in 2 tablespoons of the oil. Transfer meat to a slow cooker.

3. Layer in slow cooker, in order, carrots, celery and olives. DO NOT STIR.

4. In skillet, sauté onion and garlic for 2 minutes, adding additional oil if needed. Stir in stewed tomatoes with juice, wine, tomato paste, basil, thyme, salt and pepper. Stirring, bring to a boil. Pour over vegetables in slow cooker.

5. Cover and cook on high for 3½ to 4 hours or on low for 7 to 8 hours or until meat and vegetables are tender.

6. Stir in zucchini or peas. Immediately cover and cook on high for 20 to 30 minutes or until zucchini or peas are tender.

Serve with crusty sourdough rolls and red wine.

High setting		**Low setting**
3½ to 4 hours		**7 to 8 hours**

CHARLIE'S BURGUNDY BEEF

Makes 6 servings

Preparation Time: 10 minutes
Slow Cooker Cooking Time: 4 to 4½ hours on high or 8 to 9 hours on low
Last-Minute Cooking Time: none

> 1 **boneless beef chuck pot roast (2¼ to 2½ lb.)**
> 1 **can (10¾ oz.) condensed beef mushroom soup**
> 1 **can (10¾ oz.) condensed creamy onion soup**
> 1 **cup sliced mushrooms or chopped onion (optional)**
> ¼ **cup burgundy wine**

1. Trim excess fat from meat. Cut meat into 1-inch pieces. Place in a slow cooker.

2. Stir in soups, mushrooms or onion if desired, and wine. Scrape down sides of slow cooker.

3. Cover and cook on high for 4 to 4½ hours or on low for 8 to 9 hours or until very tender.

Serve with noodles and French-cut green beans.

High setting
4 to 4½ hours

Low setting
8 to 9 hours

ITALIAN VEGETABLE SOUP

(pictured on page 26)

Makes 4 hearty servings

Preparation Time: 20 minutes
Slow Cooker Cooking Time: 4 to 4½ hours on high or 8 to 9 hours on low
Last-Minute Cooking Time: 10 to 15 minutes on high

>   3 **small carrots, thinly sliced**
>   1 **small onion, chopped**
>   2 **ribs celery, sliced**
>   2 **small potatoes, diced**
>   2 **tablespoons chopped parsley**
>   1 **large clove garlic, minced**
>   3 **teaspoons beef bouillon granules**
>   1¼ **teaspoons dried basil leaves, crushed**
>   ½ **teaspoon salt**
>   ¼ **teaspoon pepper**
>   1 **can (15 oz.) red kidney beans**
>   3 **cups water**
>   1 **can (8 oz.) stewed tomatoes, cut up and**
>   **juice reserved**
>   1 **cup diced cooked ham**

1. Layer in a slow cooker, in order, carrots, onion, celery, potatoes, parsley, garlic, bouillon granules, basil, salt, pepper and kidney beans with liquid. Add water. DO NOT STIR.

2. Cover and cook on high for 4 to 4½ hours or on low for 8 to 9 hours or until vegetables are tender.

3. Stir in stewed tomatoes with juice and ham. Immediately cover and cook on high for 10 to 15 minutes or until heated through.

Serve with grated Parmesan cheese. If desired, serve over cooked pasta in bottom of soup bowls.

High setting
4 to 4½ hours

Low setting
8 to 9 hours

KENTUCKY BURGOO

Makes 10 to 12 servings

Preparation Time: 20 minutes
Slow Cooker Cooking Time: 4 to 4½ hours on high or 8 to 9 hours on low
Last-Minute Cooking Time: 30 minutes on high

1 **pound lean beef stew meat**
1 **pound lean pork stew meat or chops,**
   cut in 1-inch pieces
1 **teaspoon onion salt**
½ **teaspoon pepper**
¼ **teaspoon ground red pepper**
3 **carrots, sliced**
1 **medium onion, chopped**
4 **chicken thighs, skinned**
2 **small red potatoes, peeled if desired and cubed**
1 **cup chopped green pepper**
1 **can (14½ oz.) stewed tomatoes, cut up and**
   juice reserved
1 **can (10¾ oz.) double-strength chicken broth**
1 **can (17 oz.) whole kernel corn**
1 **can (17 oz.) baby lima beans, drained**

1. Place beef and pork in a 6-quart slow cooker. Sprinkle with onion salt, pepper and red pepper. Toss until evenly coated.

2. Layer in slow cooker, in order, carrots, onion, chicken, potatoes, green pepper and stewed tomatoes with juice. Add chicken broth. Pour liquid from corn into slow cooker; set corn aside. DO NOT STIR mixture in slow cooker.

3. Cover and cook on high for 4 to 4½ hours or on low for 8 to 9 hours or until beef, pork and vegetables are tender.

4. Remove chicken. Stir corn and lima beans into mixture in slow cooker. Cook on high for 30 minutes or until heated through.

5. Meanwhile, when cool enough to handle, remove chicken from bones and cut into bite-size pieces. Discard bones. Return chicken to mixture and heat through.

Serve with garlic bread.

High setting
4 to 4½ hours

Low setting
8 to 9 hours

MOCK BEEF BURGUNDY

Makes 4 to 5 servings

Preparation Time: 25 minutes
Slow Cooker Cooking Time: 4 to 5 hours on high or 8 to 10 hours on low
Last-Minute Cooking Time: none

> 2 **pounds lean beef stew meat, cut in 1-inch pieces**
> 1/3 **cup all-purpose flour**
> 1½ **teaspoons salt**
> ½ **teaspoon dried thyme leaves, crushed**
> ¼ **teaspoon pepper**
> ¼ **teaspoon garlic powder**
> 3 **carrots, cut in ½-inch slices**
> 1 **medium onion, chopped**
> ½ **pound mushrooms, cut in half**
> ½ **cup boiling water**
> 2 **teaspoons beef bouillon granules**
> 1 **vegetable bouillon cube, crumbled**
> 1 **cup cranberry juice**
> ½ **large bay leaf**

1. Place meat in a slow cooker. Sprinkle with flour, salt, thyme, pepper and garlic powder. Toss to coat meat. Add carrots, onion and mushrooms.

2. In a small bowl, stir water, beef bouillon granules and vegetable bouillon until bouillon is dissolved. Pour over vegetables. Add cranberry juice. Tuck bay leaf into center. DO NOT STIR.

3. Cover and cook on high for 4 to 5 hours or on low for 8 to 10 hours or until meat and vegetables are tender. Remove bay leaf.

Serve with steamed rice and spinach.

High setting		Low setting
4 to 5 hours		8 to 10 hours

Pictured on following page: Polish Kraut 'n' Apples (see page 16).

MILWAUKEE SHORT RIBS

Makes 4 servings

Preparation Time: 10 minutes
Slow Cooker Cooking Time: 4 to 5 hours on high or 8 to 10 hours on low
Last-Minute Cooking Time: about 5 minutes on stovetop

> 3 **medium onions, each cut in 8 wedges**
> 8 **beef short ribs (3 to 3½ lb. total)**
> 1 **large bay leaf**
> 1 **can (12 oz.) beer**
> 2 **tablespoons brown sugar**
> 2 **tablespoons Dijon mustard**
> 2 **tablespoons tomato paste**
> 2 **teaspoons beef bouillon granules**
> 1 **teaspoon dried thyme leaves, crushed**
> 1 **teaspoon salt**
> ¼ **teaspoon pepper**
> ⅓ **cup water**
> 3 **tablespoons all-purpose flour**

1. Place onions in bottom of a slow cooker. Arrange short ribs on top and tuck bay leaf into center. Pour 1 cup of the beer over meat.

2. In a small bowl, stir remaining beer, brown sugar, Dijon mustard, tomato paste, bouillon granules, thyme, salt and pepper until smooth. Pour mixture over meat.

3. Cover and cook on high for 4 to 5 hours or on low for 8 to 10 hours or until meat is tender.

4. Transfer meat and onions to a platter. Cover and keep warm. Skim fat from broth. Pour 2 cups of the broth into a small saucepan.

5. In a jar, shake water and flour until smooth; stir into broth. Stirring over medium-high heat, bring to a boil and boil until thickened.

6. To serve, spoon some sauce over meat and onions. Serve remaining sauce separately.

Serve with poppy seed noodles, buttered carrots and cole slaw.

High setting		Low setting
4 to 5 hours		8 to 10 hours

Pictured on preceding page: Ribs and Limas (see page 57).

COUNTRY-STYLE PEA SOUP

Makes 12 (1½-cup) servings

Preparation Time: 10 minutes
Slow Cooker Cooking Time: 4 to 5 hours on high or 8 to 10 hours on low
Last-Minute Cooking Time: 30 minutes on high

- 2 **packages (16 oz. each) dried green split peas**
  (4 cups total)
- 3 **meaty ham hocks, split (about 3 lb. total)**
- 4 **small carrots, peeled and thinly sliced**
- 2 **medium onions, chopped**
- 2 **ribs celery, thinly sliced**
- 2 or 3 **cloves garlic, minced**
- 2 **medium bay leaves**
- 2 **teaspoons salt**
- ¼ **teaspoon pepper**
- 3 **quarts hot water**
- 1 **quart hot milk or half-and-half**
  Croutons (optional)

1. Layer in a slow cooker, in order, peas, ham hocks, carrots, onions, celery, garlic, bay leaves, salt and pepper. Pour in water. DO NOT STIR.

2. Cover and cook on high for 4 to 5 hours or on low for 8 to 10 hours or until peas are very soft and ham hocks are tender.

3. Remove ham hocks and bay leaves. If you prefer a smoother soup, cool slightly, then purée the vegetable mixture, 2 to 3 cups at a time, in a blender container. Cut meat from bone; dice and return ham to soup in slow cooker.

4. Stir in milk. Cover and cook on high for 30 minutes or until heated through.

5. Ladle into soup bowls; garnish with croutons, if desired.

Serve with corn bread and fresh fruit.

NOTE: Soup can be made ahead through Step 4. Cool, then cover and refrigerate up to 2 days. To reheat, transfer to a large saucepan and cook over medium-low heat for 15 to 20 minutes, stirring occasionally. Soup can be frozen up to 1 month. Thaw in refrigerator before reheating.

High setting
4 to 5 hours

Low setting
8 to 10 hours

ORIENTAL PORK ROAST

Makes 6 servings

Preparation Time: 15 minutes
Slow Cooker Cooking Time: 4½ to 5 hours on high or 9 to 10 hours on low
Last-Minute Cooking Time: none

> 1 pork shoulder blade roast (4 to 4½ lb.)
> 1½ teaspoons five-spice powder*
> 2 tablespoons vegetable oil
> ¼ cup sliced green onions
> 2 tablespoons sesame seeds
> 2 cloves garlic, minced
> ¾ cup water
> ½ cup dry vermouth or white wine
> 3 tablespoons soy sauce
> 2 teaspoons chicken bouillon granules
> ⅓ cup cold water
> 3 tablespoons cornstarch

1. Rub roast with five-spice powder. In a 4-quart Dutch oven or large heavy skillet over medium-high heat, brown meat on all sides in oil. Transfer meat to a slow cooker.

2. In remaining oil in Dutch oven, sauté green onions, sesame seeds and garlic for 1 minute; remove from heat. Add ¾ cup water, vermouth, soy sauce and bouillon granules. Stir to loosen browned bits from bottom. Pour mixture over roast in slow cooker.

3. Cover and cook on high for 4½ to 5 hours or on low for 9 to 10 hours or until meat is very tender.

4. Transfer roast to a platter; cover and keep warm. Skim fat from broth. Pour broth into a medium saucepan (you will have about 2¾ cups). Over medium heat, bring to a boil.

5. Meanwhile, in a small bowl, stir ⅓ cup cold water and cornstarch until smooth. Stir into broth. Stirring over medium heat, bring to a boil and boil for 1 to 2 minutes or until thickened.

6. To serve, carve meat and spoon some sauce over. Serve remaining sauce separately.

Serve with Oriental noodles and Chinese pea pods.

*Five-spice powder may be found in the seasonings or Oriental section of your supermarket.

High setting   **Low setting**
4½ to 5 hours   **9 to 10 hours**

HUNGARIAN STEW

Makes 6 servings

Preparation Time: 15 to 20 minutes
Slow Cooker Cooking Time: 4½ to 5 hours on high or 9 to 10 hours on low
Last-Minute Cooking Time: none

½ cup all-purpose flour
1 teaspoon paprika
1 teaspoon garlic salt
¼ teaspoon pepper
3 pounds lean beef chuck short ribs*
3 tablespoons solid vegetable shortening
4 carrots, cut in 2-inch pieces
2 small onions, cut in wedges
4 ribs celery, cut in 2-inch pieces
1 small green pepper, diced
1 cup water
1 can (6 oz.) tomato paste
3 teaspoons beef bouillon granules
2 teaspoons dried basil leaves, crushed
½ teaspoon dried thyme leaves, crushed

1. In a plastic bag, mix flour, paprika, garlic salt and pepper.

2. Trim excess fat from meat. Toss meat in flour mixture, a few pieces at a time, and shake until meat is well coated. Reserve remaining flour mixture.

3. In a large skillet over medium heat, brown meat in shortening. Transfer meat to a slow cooker. Top with carrots, onions, celery and green pepper. DO NOT STIR.

4. Pour off excess drippings from skillet. Stirring over medium heat, brown remaining flour mixture. Remove skillet from heat. Stir in water, tomato paste, bouillon granules, basil and thyme until smooth, scraping to loosen browned bits from bottom of skillet. Pour over meat and vegetables.

5. Cover and cook on high for 4½ to 5 hours or on low for 9 to 10 hours or until meat and vegetables are very tender.

Serve with biscuits or corn bread.

*Or use 3 pounds lean beef oxtails, cut in 1½- to 2-inch pieces.

High setting
4½ to 5 hours

Low setting
9 to 10 hours

ENGLISH BEEF WITH A TWIST

Makes 6 servings

Preparation Time: 10 minutes
Slow Cooker Cooking Time: 4½ to 5 hours on high or 9 to 10 hours on low
Last-Minute Cooking Time: 15 minutes on high

- 1 **boneless beef top round steak (about 1½ lb.)**
- 1 **medium onion, chopped**
- 1 **can (10½ oz.) double-strength beef broth**
- 1 **tablespoon steak sauce or Worcestershire sauce**
- 1 **tablespoon catsup**
- 1 **teaspoon curry powder**
- ½ **teaspoon ground ginger**
- ½ **teaspoon salt**
- ¼ **teaspoon pepper**
- ½ **cup dairy sour cream**
- 2 **tablespoons prepared horseradish**
- 1½ **tablespoons cornstarch**
  Sliced chives or chopped parsley

1. Trim excess fat from meat. Cut meat into serving-size pieces or cubes. Place meat and onion in a slow cooker; stir to combine.

2. In a medium bowl, stir beef broth, steak sauce, catsup, curry powder, ginger, salt and pepper until blended. Pour over meat.

3. Cover and cook on high for 4½ to 5 hours or on low for 9 to 10 hours or until meat is very tender.

4. In a small bowl, stir sour cream, horseradish and cornstarch until blended. Stir into liquid around meat. Cover and cook on high for 15 minutes or until thickened. Garnish with chives.

Serve with rice pilaf and broccoli spears.

High setting	Low setting
4½ to 5 hours	**9 to 10 hours**

FAMILY POT ROAST

Makes 8 servings

Preparation Time: 10 minutes
Slow Cooker Cooking Time: 4½ to 5 hours on high or 9 to 10 hours on low
Last-Minute Cooking Time: 20 to 30 minutes on high

- 1 **boneless beef chuck roast (3 to 4 lb.)**
- 1 **cup sliced celery**
- 1 **cup chopped onion**
- 1 **can (10¾ oz.) condensed tomato soup or**
    cream of mushroom soup
- 1 **tablespoon vinegar**
- 2 **teaspoons beef bouillon granules**
- 2 **teaspoons dried sage leaves, crushed**
- ¼ **teaspoon pepper**
- ½ **cup cold water**
- ⅓ **cup all-purpose flour**

1. Trim excess fat from meat. Place roast in a slow cooker, cutting in half if needed to fit. Add celery and onion.

2. In a medium bowl, stir soup, vinegar, bouillon granules, sage and pepper. Pour into slow cooker.

3. Cover and cook on high for 4½ to 5 hours or on low for 9 to 10 hours or until meat is very tender.

4. In a small bowl, stir water and flour until smooth. Stir into boiling liquid around roast. Cover and cook on high for 20 to 30 minutes or until thickened.

5. Transfer meat to a warm platter. Serve gravy separately.

Serve with hashed brown potatoes and Brussels sprouts.

High setting
4½ to 5 hours

Low setting
9 to 10 hours

BUFFET BEEF WITH ARTICHOKES

Makes 8 servings

Preparation Time: 15 minutes
Slow Cooker Cooking Time: 4½ to 5 hours on high or 9 to 10 hours on low
Last-Minute Cooking Time: 30 minutes on high

- 1 **boneless beef chuck roast (about 2½ lb.)**
- 2 **medium onions, quartered and sliced**
- 3 **tablespoons all-purpose flour**
- 3 **cloves garlic, minced**
- 1 **teaspoon dried dill weed or thyme leaves, crushed**
- ½ **teaspoon salt**
- ½ **teaspoon pepper**
- 1 **can (10½ oz.) double-strength beef broth or**
     1¼ cups dry red wine
- ¼ **cup water**
- 1 **package (0.87 oz.) brown gravy mix**
- 1 **package (9 oz.) frozen artichoke hearts,**
     thawed and cut if large
- ½ **pound mushrooms, quartered**

1. Trim excess fat from meat. Cut meat into bite-size pieces. Place meat, onions, flour, garlic, dill, salt and pepper in a slow cooker. Toss to coat. Add broth.

2. Cover and cook on high for 4½ to 5 hours or on low for 9 to 10 hours or until meat is very tender.

3. In a small bowl, stir water and gravy mix until smooth. Quickly stir gravy mixture, artichoke hearts and mushrooms into meat mixture.

4. Cover and cook on high for 30 minutes or until thickened and vegetables are tender.

Serve with noodles or biscuits.

High setting
4½ to 5 hours

Low setting
9 to 10 hours

PACIFIC RIBS

Makes 4 servings

Preparation Time: 10 minutes
Slow Cooker Cooking Time: 5 to 5½ hours on high or 10 to 11 hours on low
Last-Minute Cooking Time: 3 to 5 minutes under broiler (optional)

> 8 **lean country-style pork spareribs (about 3½ lb.)**
> 1 **can (6 oz.) tomato juice or vegetable juice cocktail**
>   **(¾ cup)**
> 3 **tablespoons soy sauce**
> 2 **tablespoons dried minced onion**
> 1 **tablespoon minced fresh gingerroot**
> 1 **tablespoon honey**
> 2 **cloves garlic, minced**
> 1 **teaspoon ground coriander**
> ½ **teaspoon ground cumin**
>   **Dash of ground cloves**

1. Trim excess fat from ribs. Place four ribs in a slow cooker.

2. In a medium bowl, stir tomato juice, soy sauce, onion, gingerroot, honey, garlic, coriander, cumin and cloves. Pour half of the mixture over ribs in slow cooker. Add remaining ribs and pour over remaining tomato juice mixture.

3. Cover and cook on high for 5 to 5½ hours or on low for 10 to 11 hours or until very tender.

4. If desired, transfer ribs to a foil-lined jelly roll pan and arrange in a single layer. Baste with cooking liquid. Broil 6 inches from heat source for 3 to 5 minutes or until browned. Baste again with cooking liquid before serving.

Serve with sweet potatoes and fresh pineapple.

High setting		Low setting
5 to 5½ hours		10 to 11 hours

SAUERBRATEN

Makes 10 to 12 servings

Preparation Time: 10 minutes plus 12 hours or overnight for marinating
Slow Cooker Cooking Time: 5 to 5½ hours on high or 10 to 11 hours on low
Last-Minute Cooking Time: about 10 minutes on stovetop

- 1 **medium onion, sliced**
- 1 **boneless beef rump roast (about 4 lb.)**
- 1½ **cups dry red wine**
- ¾ **cup cider vinegar**
- 2 **tablespoons sugar**
- 2 **bay leaves**
- 8 **whole cloves**
- 1 **teaspoon salt**
- ½ **teaspoon pepper**
- ½ **teaspoon dried thyme leaves, crushed**
- 1 **can (10½ oz.) double-strength beef broth**
- ⅓ **cup cold water**
- ¼ **cup cornstarch**
- 1 **teaspoon ground ginger (optional)**

1. Place half of the onion in a deep 2½- to 3-quart bowl. Slash top layer of fat on roast in a crisscross pattern. Place roast in bowl. Top with remaining onion; set aside.

2. In a small saucepan, place wine, vinegar, sugar, bay leaves, cloves, salt, pepper and thyme. Over medium heat, bring to a boil. Pour over roast, pushing bay leaves into liquid. Cover and refrigerate at least 12 hours or overnight, turning several times.

3. Transfer roast to a slow cooker, fat-side up. With a slotted spoon, transfer onions to slow cooker. Add beef broth and 1 cup of the marinade; discard remaining marinade.

4. Cover and cook on high for 5 to 5½ hours or on low for 10 to 11 hours or until roast is very tender. Transfer roast and onions to a large platter. Cover and keep warm.

5. Pour 3 cups of the cooking liquid into a medium saucepan; discard remaining cooking liquid. Over medium heat, bring to a boil.

6. Meanwhile, in a small bowl, stir cold water, cornstarch and ginger until smooth. Stir into boiling liquid. Stirring, bring to a boil and boil for 1 to 2 minutes or until thickened. Serve gravy separately.

Serve with potato cakes, Italian green beans and apple salad.

NOTE: Leftover roast can be sliced for sandwiches.

High setting	**Low setting**
5 to 5½ hours	**10 to 11 hours**

OVERNIGHT BEAN SOUP

Makes 6 to 8 servings

Preparation Time: 1¼ hours or overnight
Slow Cooker Cooking Time: 5 to 5½ hours on high or 10 to 11 hours on low
Last-Minute Cooking Time: 15 minutes on high

    1 **pound dried small white beans**
    6 **cups water**
    2 **cups boiling water**
    2 **large carrots, diced**
    3 **ribs celery, diced**
    2 **teaspoons chicken bouillon granules**
    1 **bay leaf**
  ½ **teaspoon dried thyme leaves, crushed**
  ½ **teaspoon salt**
  ¼ **teaspoon pepper**
  ¼ **cup chopped fresh parsley**
    1 **package (about 1.25 oz.) dry onion soup mix**
       Fried bacon, crumbled (optional)

1. Rinse beans; discard any damaged beans and stones. Place beans in a 3-quart saucepan with 6 cups water. Over medium-high heat, bring to a boil; reduce heat to low and simmer for 2 minutes. Remove from heat. Cover and let stand for 1 hour or overnight.

2. If desired, drain liquid into a measuring cup, then discard; add same amount of fresh water to beans. (Some nutrients will be lost.) Transfer beans and water to a slow cooker. Add boiling water, carrots, celery, bouillon granules, bay leaf, thyme, salt and pepper.

3. Cover and cook on high for 5 to 5½ hours or on low for 10 to 11 hours or until beans are very tender.

4. Stir in parsley and soup mix. Cover and cook on high for 15 minutes or until heated through and onion and parsley are tender.

5. Remove bay leaf. Ladle 2 cups of the soup mixture into a blender container. Cover and blend until puréed. Stir into soup mixture in slow cooker and serve. Garnish with bacon if desired.

Serve with grilled cheese sandwiches and sliced fresh fruit.

HIGH ALTITUDE ADJUSTMENTS: At 6,000 feet, simmer beans for 10 minutes in Step 1. For best results, let stand overnight before cooking in slow cooker. Cooking will take longer, as much as 7 hours total on high or 14 hours total on low.

      High setting   **Low setting**
     5 to 5½ hours   **10 to 11 hours**

BEEF 'N' VEGETABLE SOUP

Makes 12 (1-cup) servings

Preparation Time: 15 minutes
Slow Cooker Cooking Time: 5 to 5½ hours on high or 10 to 11 hours on low
Last-Minute Cooking Time: 30 minutes on high

- 1½ pounds sliced lean beef shanks
- 1 tablespoon vegetable oil
- 1½ cups chopped onions
- 1 cup chopped carrots
- ½ cup chopped celery
- 8 cups water
- 1 can (14½ oz.) stewed tomatoes, cut up and juice reserved
- ¾ cup pearl barley
- 2 tablespoons beef bouillon granules
- 2 teaspoons Worcestershire sauce
- 1½ teaspoons dried basil leaves, crushed
- 2 cloves garlic, minced
- ¼ teaspoon pepper
- 10 medium mushrooms, sliced

1. In a 10-inch skillet over medium-high heat, brown beef shanks in oil. Transfer to a slow cooker.

2. Add to slow cooker, in order, onions, carrots, celery, water, stewed tomatoes with juice, barley, bouillon granules, Worcestershire sauce, basil, garlic and pepper. DO NOT STIR.

3. Cover and cook on high for 5 to 5½ hours or on low for 10 to 11 hours or until meat is tender.

4. Remove beef shanks from slow cooker; set aside until cool enough to handle. Cool mixture slightly. Skim off fat. Add mushrooms to slow cooker. Cut meat from bone; dice and return meat to soup in slow cooker. Cover and cook on high for 30 minutes or until heated through.

Serve with saltine crackers or fruit muffins.

NOTE: Soup can be made ahead through cutting the meat off the bone in Step 4. Cool, then cover and refrigerate up to 2 days. To reheat, transfer to a large saucepan and cook over medium heat for 15 to 20 minutes, stirring occasionally. Soup can be frozen up to 2 months. Thaw in refrigerator before reheating.

High setting **Low setting**
5 to 5½ hours **10 to 11 hours**

FRENCH DIP ROAST

Makes 8 to 10 servings

Preparation Time: 10 minutes
Slow Cooker Cooking Time: 5 to 6 hours on high or 10 to 12 hours on low
Last-Minute Cooking Time: none

1 **large onion, quartered and sliced**
1 **beef bottom round roast (about 3 lb.)**
½ **cup dry white wine or water**
1 **package (¾ oz.) au jus gravy mix**
⅛ **teaspoon seasoned pepper**

1. Place onion in a slow cooker.

2. Trim excess fat from roast. Cut meat in half if needed to fit in slow cooker. Place in slow cooker.

3. In a small bowl, stir wine, au jus mix and seasoned pepper until blended. Pour over roast.

4. Cover and cook on high for 5 to 6 hours or on low for 10 to 12 hours or until very tender.

5. Remove meat from liquid. Let stand for 5 minutes before thinly slicing across grain. Strain broth if desired; taste for salt.

Serve with hard French rolls to make sandwiches, adding onions if desired. Use liquid for dipping.

NOTE: If not serving immediately, sliced meat and broth can be held on low in the slow cooker up to 1 hour.

High setting   **Low setting**
5 to 6 hours   **10 to 12 hours**

RIBS AND LIMAS

(pictured on page 44)

Makes 6 servings

Preparation Time: 20 minutes
Slow Cooker Cooking Time: 5 to 6 hours on high or 10 to 12 hours on low
Last-Minute Cooking Time: 20 to 30 minutes on high

- 3 **pounds lean beef short ribs**
- 2 **tablespoons vegetable oil**
- 1 **medium onion, chopped**
- 4 **medium carrots, sliced**
- ¼ **cup packed brown sugar**
- 2 **tablespoons all-purpose flour**
- 2 **teaspoons dry mustard**
- 1½ **teaspoons salt**
- ¼ **teaspoon pepper**
- 1¼ **cups water**
- ¼ **cup cider vinegar**
- 1 **large bay leaf, broken in half**
- 1 **package (10 oz.) frozen lima beans,***
  cooked according to package directions

1. Trim excess fat from ribs. Cut ribs in serving-size pieces if large. In a large skillet over medium heat, brown ribs in oil; discard drippings.

2. Meanwhile, place onion and carrots in a slow cooker. Add ribs.

3. In a medium bowl, stir brown sugar, flour, dry mustard, salt and pepper until blended. Stir in water and vinegar until smooth. Pour over ribs. Push bay leaf into liquid.

4. Cover and cook on high for 5 to 6 hours or on low for 10 to 12 hours or until meat is very tender.

5. Stir in lima beans. Immediately cover and cook on high for 20 to 30 minutes or until heated through.

6. Remove bay leaf before serving.

Serve with a citrus salad and crusty rolls.

*Or use a 10-oz. package frozen peas, thawed.

High setting
5 to 6 hours

Low setting
10 to 12 hours

"SMOKED" BRISKET

Makes 6 to 8 servings

Preparation Time: 10 minutes
Slow Cooker Cooking Time: 5½ to 6 hours on high or 11 to 12 hours on low
Last-Minute Cooking Time: none

- 1 **medium onion, sliced**
- 1 **lean beef brisket (about 2½ lb.)**
- 1 **to 1½ tablespoons liquid smoke**
- 1 **teaspoon seasoned salt**
- ½ **teaspoon pepper**
- ¼ **cup catsup**
- 2 **teaspoons prepared mustard**
- ½ **teaspoon celery seeds**

1. Place onion in a slow cooker.

2. Trim excess fat from meat. Cut brisket in half if needed to fit in slow cooker. Rub all surfaces of meat with liquid smoke, seasoned salt and pepper. Place meat in slow cooker.

3. In a small bowl, stir catsup, mustard and celery seeds until blended. Spread over top of meat.

4. Cover and cook on high for 5½ to 6 hours or on low for 11 to 12 hours or until meat is very tender.

5. To serve, slice meat diagonally. Serve onions and juices separately if desired.

Serve with baked beans, pickles and onion rolls.

High setting
5½ to 6 hours

Low setting
11 to 12 hours

BRISKET FOR A CROWD

Makes 10 to 12 servings

Preparation Time: 10 minutes
Slow Cooker Cooking Time: 8 to 9 hours on low
Last-Minute Cooking Time: about 10 minutes on stovetop (optional)

1   beef brisket (4½ to 5 lb.)
2   tablespoons vegetable oil
1   envelope (about 1.25 oz.) dried onion soup mix
1   cup chopped celery
1   cup chopped onion
1   cup chili sauce
½   cup water
1   can (12 oz.) beer or 1½ cups beef bouillon
3   tablespoons butter or margarine (optional)
3   tablespoons all-purpose flour (optional)
     Salt and pepper (optional)

1. Cut meat in half if needed to fit in skillet and slow cooker. In a large skillet over medium-high heat, brown both sides of brisket in oil. Place meat in a slow cooker. Discard drippings.

2. Sprinkle onion soup mix over meat. Top with celery and onion. In a small bowl, mix chili sauce and water; pour over vegetables. Pour beer around meat.

3. Cover and cook on low for 8 to 9 hours or until meat is fork tender.

4. If time allows, cool meat in liquid, about 1 hour.

5. Skim off fat from cooking liquid. Remove meat and thinly slice diagonally across the grain. Use cold for sandwiches. Or, place meat in a large saucepan, cover with cooking liquid and reheat over low heat for 10 to 30 minutes (depending on amount of meat). Serve with gravy if desired.

6. To make gravy: In a medium saucepan over medium heat, melt butter. Add flour. Cook and stir for 1 minute. Add 2 cups cooking liquid. Stirring, bring to a boil and boil until thickened. Taste gravy for seasoning and add salt and pepper if needed. For a thinner gravy, add more liquid. Serve with meat.

Serve with boiled potatoes.

High setting not recommended   **Low setting 8 to 9 hours**

WRANGLER'S POT ROAST

Makes 8 servings

Preparation Time: 15 minutes
Slow Cooker Cooking Time: 9 to 10 hours on low
Last-Minute Cooking Time: 10 to 15 minutes on high

> 1 **boneless lean beef chuck roast (about 4 lb.)**
> 1 **teaspoon salt**
> ¼ **teaspoon pepper**
> 2 **tablespoons vegetable oil**
> 1 **large onion, chopped**
> 8 **large cloves garlic, crushed**
> ¾ **cup dry red wine or beef broth**
> 2 **to 3 teaspoons instant coffee granules**
> 1 **bay leaf**
> 3 **tablespoons cold water**
> 2 **tablespoons cornstarch**

1. Sprinkle roast with salt and pepper and rub in. Cut roast in half if needed to fit in a slow cooker.

2. In a large skillet over medium heat, brown roast in oil. Transfer roast to slow cooker.

3. Sauté onion and garlic in skillet until lightly browned. Add wine and coffee granules. Cook over medium heat, stirring to loosen browned bits from bottom of skillet. Pour over meat. Push bay leaf into liquid.

4. Cover and cook on low for 9 to 10 hours or until meat is very tender.

5. Using a slotted spoon, remove bay leaf and garlic. Transfer meat to a heated platter. Cover and keep warm.

6. In a small bowl, stir cold water and cornstarch until smooth. Stir into hot liquid in slow cooker. Cover and cook on high heat for 10 to 15 minutes or until boiling and thickened.

7. Slice meat and serve with gravy.

Serve with boiled or mashed potatoes and corn-on-the-cob.

**High setting not
recommended**

**Low setting
9 to 10 hours**

INDEX
*recipes photographed